Fun and Simple

Western State Crafts

Montana, Wyoming, Idaho, Utah, and Nevada

June Ponte

Enslow Elementary

an imprint of

Enslow Publishers, Inc.

40 Industrial Road
Box 398
Berkeley Heights, NJ 07922
USA

http://www.enslow.com

This book meets the National Council for the Social Studies standards.

Enslow Elementary, an imprint of Enslow Publishers, Inc.

Enslow Elementary® is a registered trademark of Enslow Publishers, Inc.

Copyright © 2009 by Enslow Publishers, Inc.

Library of Congress Cataloging-in-Publication Data

Ponte, June.
  Fun and simple Western state crafts : Montana, Wyoming, Idaho, Utah, and Nevada / June Ponte.
    p. cm. — (Fun and simple state crafts)
  Includes bibliographical references and index.
  Summary: "Provides facts and craft ideas for each of the states that make up the Western region of the United States"—Provided by publisher.
  ISBN-13: 978-0-7660-2985-9
  ISBN-10: 0-7660-2985-9
  1. Handicraft—West (U.S.)—Juvenile literature. I. Title.
  TT23.6.P65 2008
  745.5—dc22

                                              2008018408

Printed in the United States of America

10 9 8 7 6 5 4 3 2 1

To Our Readers:
We have done our best to make sure all Internet Addresses in this book were active and appropriate when we went to press. However, the author and the publisher have no control over and assume no liability for the material available on those Internet sites or on other Web sites they may link to. Any comments or suggestions can be sent by e-mail to comments@enslow.com or to the address on the back cover.

Every effort has been made to locate all copyright holders of material used in this book. If any errors or omissions have occurred, corrections will be made in future editions of this book.

♻ Enslow Publishers, Inc., is committed to printing our books on recycled paper. The paper in every book contains 10% to 30% post-consumer waste (PCW). The cover board on the outside of each book contains 100% PCW. Our goal is to do our part to help young people and the environment too!

Illustration Credits: Crafts prepared by June Ponte; Photography by Nicole diMella/Enslow Publishers, Inc.; © 1999 Artville, LLC., pp. 6–7; © 2007 Jupiterimages, all clipart and pp. 9 (all), 15 (flower), 23 (bird), 31 (animal), 37 (flower); © 2001 Robesus, Inc., all state flags; Shutterstock, pp. 15 (tree), 23 (animal), 31 (gem), 37 (animal).

Cover Illustration: Crafts prepared by June Ponte; Photography by Nicole diMella/Enslow Publishers, Inc.; © 1999 Artville, LLC., map; © Jupiterimages, state buttons.

CONTENTS

WELCOME TO THE WESTERN STATES!

Montana, Wyoming, Idaho, Utah, and Nevada are the five states in the western region. This area is referred to as the western region because the states are located in the western area of the United States.

The geography of the western states is dramatic, and includes high plains, mountains, deserts, canyons, and valleys.

The Great Plains are in the eastern part of Montana, where the Missouri and Yellowstone rivers flow through river valleys. Montana's badlands are in the southeast, where there are many natural rock formations made by wind and water. The western part of Montana is covered by the Rocky Mountains.

The state of Wyoming is really a plateau with many tall mountain ranges. The Rocky Mountains, Great Plains, and the Intermontane Basins are Wyoming's three main land regions. An intermontane basin is a land area surrounded by or in between mountains.

Idaho is a state with many geographic variations. This state has three main land areas: the Basin and Ridge Region, the Rocky Mountains, and the Columbia Plateau.

The southeastern corner of Utah touches the corners of Colorado, Arizona, and New Mexico. This area is called the "Four Corners." The Great Salt Lake is in the northwestern corner of Utah. The Colorado Plateau, the Basin and Ridge Region, and the Rocky Mountains are Utah's three main regions.

Nevada is a state of valleys, forests, mountains, and deserts. This state has three major land areas: the Basin and Range Region, the Columbia Plateau, and the Sierra Nevada.

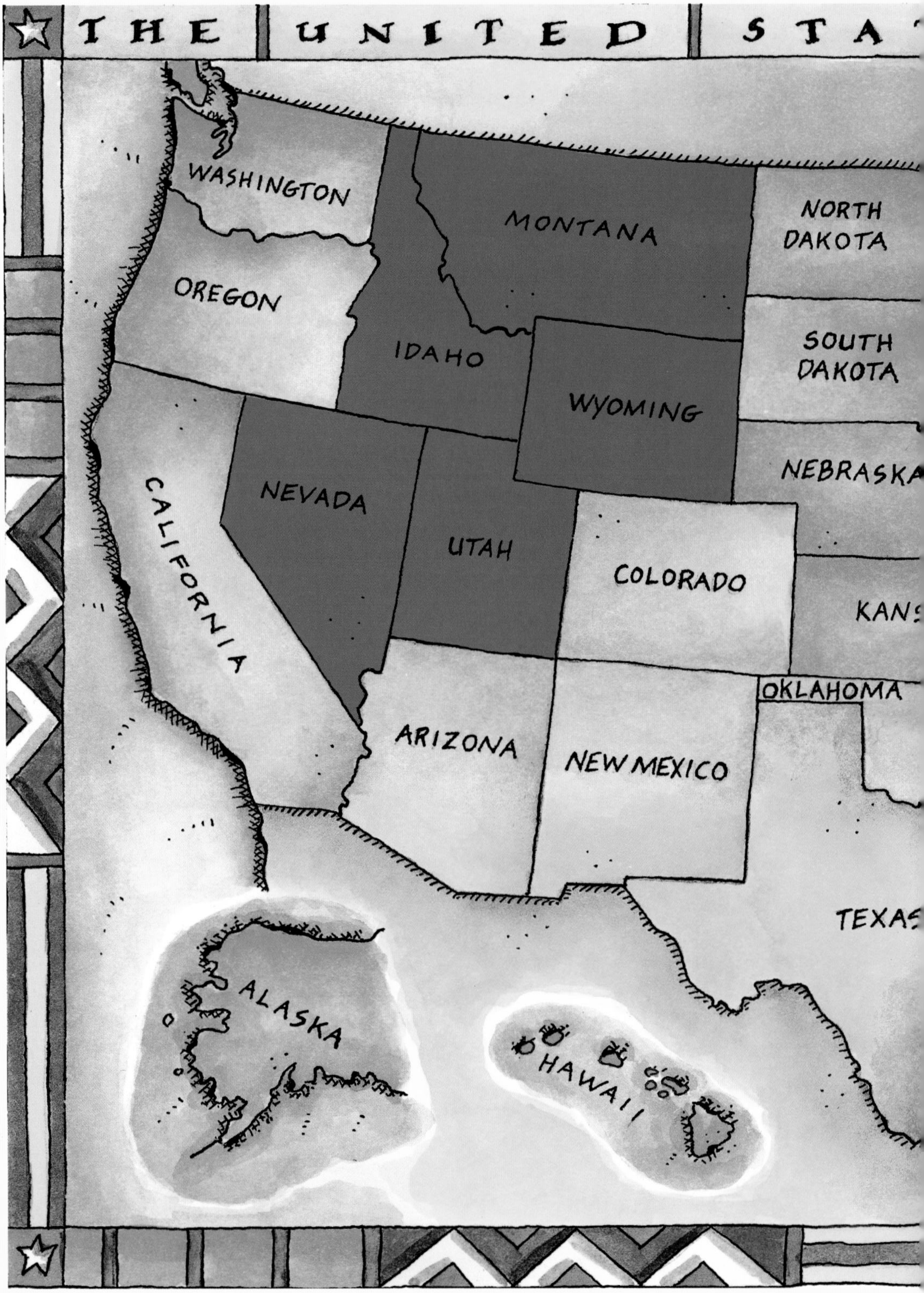
THE UNITED STA
WASHINGTON
OREGON
CALIFORNIA
NEVADA
IDAHO
MONTANA
WYOMING
UTAH
COLORADO
ARIZONA
NEW MEXICO
NORTH DAKOTA
SOUTH DAKOTA
NEBRASKA
KANS
OKLAHOMA
TEXAS
ALASKA
HAWAII

MINNESOTA

MICHIGAN

WISCONSIN

IOWA

ILLINOIS

INDIANA

OHIO

MISSOURI

KENTUCKY

WEST VIRGINIA

VIRGINIA

ARKANSAS

TENNESSEE

NORTH CAROLINA

MISSISSIPPI

ALABAMA

GEORGIA

SOUTH CAROLINA

LOUISIANA

FLORIDA

NEW HAMPSHIRE

VERMONT

MAINE

NEW YORK

MASSACHUSETTS

RHODE ISLAND

CONNECTICUT

NEW JERSEY

PENNSYLVANIA

DELAWARE

MARYLAND

WASHINGTON, D.C.

N

Western States

MONTANA

Origin of name	The state of Montana received its name from the Spanish word *montana*, which means "mountainous."
Flag	The Montana state flag is blue. The state seal appears beneath the word *Montana*, which is written in gold letters. The sun is shown rising beyond mountains, the Great Falls of the Missouri River, and forests. Mining and farming are represented by a plow, pick, and shovel. "Gold and Silver," the state motto, appears in Spanish, *Oro y Plata*, near the bottom of the seal.
Capital	Helena
Nickname	Big Sky Country and The Treasure State

Motto	*Oro y Plata* (This is a Spanish phrase which means, "Gold and Silver.")
Size (in area)	4th largest
Animal	grizzly bear
Bird	western meadowlark
Fish	blackspotted cutthroat trout
Flower	bitterroot
Gem	sapphire and Montana agate
Tree	ponderosa pine
Industry	beef cattle, wheat, barley, manufacturing of wood products and food products, mining of coal, copper, and gold

BUFFALO WALL HANGING

When early explorers looked out onto the western plains in North America, they thought that the land was "dark and moving." The explorers were actually seeing the many buffalo that once roamed the Great Plains and mountain areas. In the 1800s, so many of the animals were killed that by 1894 there were only about three hundred left. The buffalo nearly became extinct. The American Bison Society was founded in 1905 to create preserves for the animals. Preserves are places where animals can live in safety. Today, there are about 150,000 buffalo in the United States. The words *bison* and *buffalo* are used to refer to the same animal in the United States, although experts tell us that they are actually different species.

What you will need

* pencil
* poster board
* scissors
* brown fake fur
* white glue
* black permanent marker
* wiggle eye
* yarn
* clear tape

What you will do:

1. Draw a buffalo onto poster board in pencil. (See page 46 for pattern.) Cut it out.

2. Trace the poster board buffalo onto the back of the fake fur. Cut it out. Glue the fake fur to the poster board buffalo. Leave a little of the poster board showing at the bottom of the feet. Use the black marker to color in black hooves. Let dry. Glue on a wiggle eye. Let dry.

3. Tape a piece of yarn to the back to make a loop to hang the buffalo.

PLAINS INDIAN SHIELD

The Museum of the Plains Indian is in Browning, Montana. This museum has many costumes, weapons, beadwork, crafts, and toys of the Plains Indians. The Plains Indians painted their tepees, clothes, and other objects with pictures of people, antelope, horses, turtles, and other animals.

What you will need

- ☀ pencil
- ☀ poster board
- ☀ scissors
- ☀ poster paint or markers
- ☀ paintbrush
- ☀ hole punch
- ☀ yarn
- ☀ craft feathers
- ☀ clear tape

What you will do:

1. Use a pencil to draw a circle onto poster board. Cut it out (See A).

2. Draw an animal on the center of the shield (See B). Color the shield with markers or poster paint. Let dry.

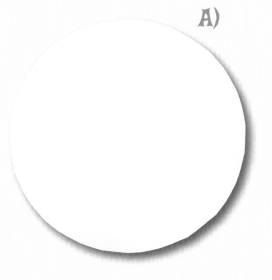
A)

3. Punch six holes around the bottom area of the shield near the edge. Tie a 6-inch piece of yarn to a feather, and thread through the hole. Repeat until all holes are threaded (See C).

B)

C)

4. Tape a piece of yarn to the back of the shield for hanging.

WYOMING

Origin of name	The name Wyoming comes from a Delaware Indian word which means "upon the great plain."
Flag	In the center of the Wyoming state flag there is a white bison, also called a buffalo, with the Great Seal of Wyoming in the center of the animal. The blue background of the flag stands for Wyoming's sky and mountains. The color white represents purity. The flag's red border stands for the American Indians living in the region and the blood of the pioneers who settled there.
Capital	Cheyenne
Nickname	The Equality State

14

Motto	"Equal Rights"
Size (in area)	10th largest
Bird	meadowlark
Fish	cutthroat trout
Flower	Indian paintbrush
Gem	jade
Tree	Plains Cottonwood
Industry	cattle, sheep, agriculture, mining, chemical products, lumber, utility and financial services, tourism

JACKALOPE STATUE

Long ago, Douglas Herrick made a fake animal that looked like a jackrabbit with antelope horns. He called it a jackalope! Cowboys sat around their campfires at night, telling stories about how the jackalope could run ninety miles an hour, and how it could imitate their voices. Some people believe that the jackalope is real, but most know it is an imaginary animal. There is an eight-foot-tall statue of a jackalope in Douglas, Wyoming.

What you will need

* self-hardening clay
* twigs
* poster paint
* paintbrush
* individual cereal box

What you will do:

1. Form a piece of self-hardening clay into a 4-inch-long egg shape.

2. Make a smaller egg shape, about 1-inch-long, for the jackalope's head. Attach the head to the larger egg-shaped body. Add four 1/2-inch bean shapes for legs. Smooth the areas where the pieces of clay meet.

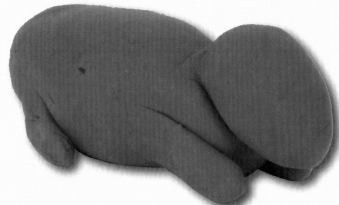

3. Make two ears for the jackalope. Make sure they are thick enough to stand up. Attach the ears to the top of the head. Leave enough room between the ears for two twigs. Make a small ball for the jackalope's tail, and attach to the body. Carefully push two small twigs into the jackalope's head, between the ears. Let dry.

4. Paint the jackalope with poster paint. Let dry. Paint the individual cereal box as you wish. Let dry. Place the jackalope on top of the cereal box to display.

DINOSAUR BONE TREASURE BOX

In 1933, Walter Boylan used dinosaur bones to build a little museum near the town of Medicine Bow, Wyoming. Today, this bone building is known as the Fossil Cabin Museum. The little museum has exhibits of dinosaur bones, rocks, and fossils. Imagine standing inside a building made of dinosaur bones!

What you will need

* pasta box (such as ziti)
* scissors
* brown felt
* white glue
* white craft foam
* green craft foam
* black permanent marker

What you will do:

1. Lay the pasta box down so that the clear plastic area is facing down. Cut along the two short edges and one long edge of the box to form a lid. Cut a small rectangular hole in the front side.

2. Cut brown felt to fit the sides and lid of the box. Glue onto the box. Let dry.

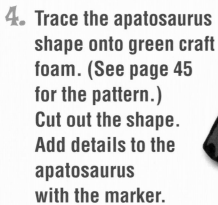

3. Trace bone shapes onto white craft foam. (See page 45 for the pattern.) Cut out enough bone shapes to cover the sides and lid of the box.

4. Trace the apatosaurus shape onto green craft foam. (See page 45 for the pattern.) Cut out the shape. Add details to the apatosaurus with the marker.

5. Glue the apatosaurus on the lid of the box. Glue the bones around the apatosaurus and on the sides of the box. Let dry.

6. Place pencils, crayons, or other small items in the box.

IDAHO

Origin of name	The name Idaho is a made-up word. The term was thought to be a Shoshone Indian word, *ee-da-how*, meaning "gem of the mountains."
Flag	The Idaho state flag is blue, edged with a gold fringe. The seal of Idaho is in the center of the flag. It shows a woman, representing liberty, equality, and justice, and a man, who is a miner. Mining, farming, and forestry, also shown on the seal, are the major industries in Idaho. The head of an elk is between the two figures, representing the wildlife in Idaho. There are two horns of plenty, called cornucopias, in front of the figures. These are symbols of abundance. *Esto perpetua* is the state motto in Latin. It appears in a scroll over the elk's head. The words "State of Idaho," in gold letters on a red and gold scroll, appear beneath the seal.

Capital	Boise
Nickname	The Gem State
Motto	Esto perpetua (This is a Latin phrase which means, "May it endure forever.")
Size (in area)	14th largest
Bird	mountain bluebird
Fish	cutthroat trout
Flower	syringa
Horse	appaloosa
Tree	white pine
Industry	potato farming, grain, tourism, cattle, sheep

CRATERS OF THE MOON DISPLAY

Thousands of years ago, molten lava poured across south central Idaho. A sixty-mile-long crack in the earth, called the Great Rift, provided a passageway for the lava to flow. Strange craters and caves formed during this time. The area is now called the Craters of the Moon National Monument and Preserve. In 1969, four American astronauts visited the monument to help them understand the kinds of surfaces they would later find on the moon.

What you will need

* self-hardening clay
* ruler
* plastic knife
* scissors
* pencil
* poster board
* colored markers

What you will do:

1. Flatten a piece of clay that is about 4 inches wide and 6 inches long. The clay should be about 1/8 inch thick. Use your thumb to make craters in the clay (See A). Make the craters different sizes. Let dry.

A)

2. Draw an astronaut on poster board (See B). (See page 45 for the pattern.) Cut it out.

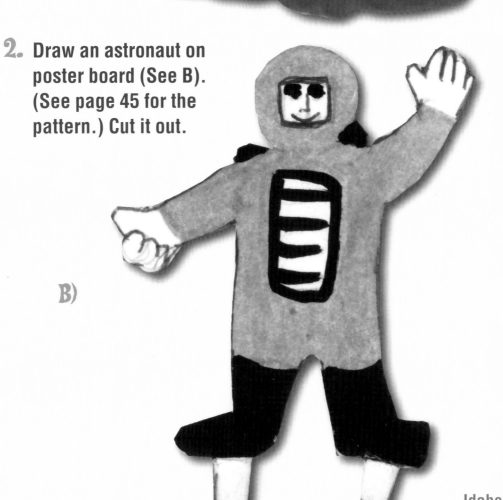

B)

3. Color the astronaut with markers. Bend the tabs on the bottom of the astronaut and place on the clay.

LITTLE WOOLY SHEEP

In autumn, the Trailing of the Sheep Festival is held in the towns of Ketchum and Hailey, Idaho. The festival celebrates the history of sheep ranching in the state. People spin wool and weave. Dancing, storytelling, food, and music are also part of the fun. Hundreds of sheep are led down Ketchum's Main Street and through the valley.

What you will need

* self-hardening clay
* poster paint
* paintbrush
* white glue
* two rhinestones or small buttons
* cotton balls
* black yarn
* red ribbon

What you will do:

1. Roll an egg-shaped piece of clay that is about 3 inches long (See A). Roll a teardrop shape for the sheep's head. Add to one end of the body. Make two oval-shaped ears. Add them to the sheep's head. Roll four legs that are about 1 inch long. Add to the underside of the body. Smooth the areas where the clay meets. Let dry.

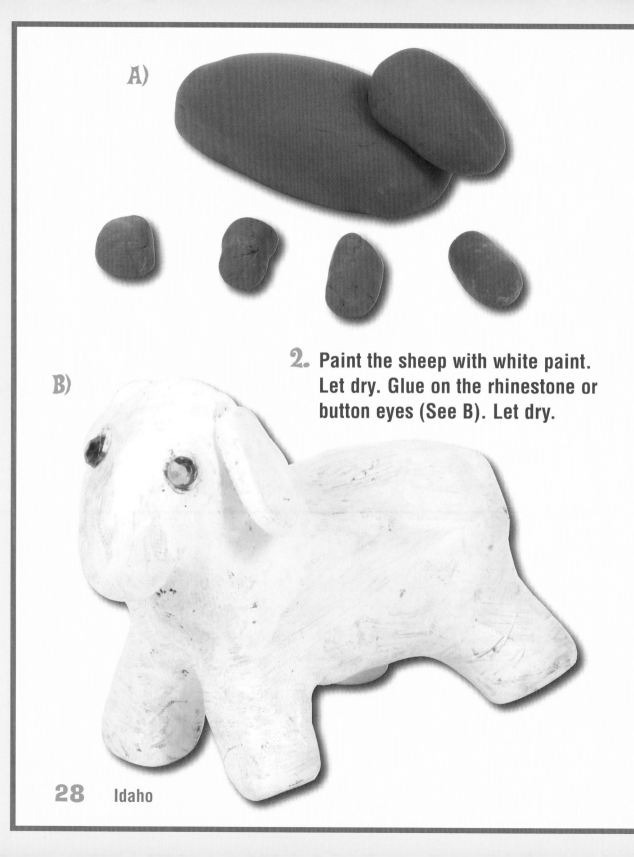

A)

B)

2. Paint the sheep with white paint. Let dry. Glue on the rhinestone or button eyes (See B). Let dry.

3. Paint the ears and nose black. Let dry. Pull apart cotton balls and glue to the body of the sheep. Add one puff of cotton for the sheep's tail. Let dry.

C)

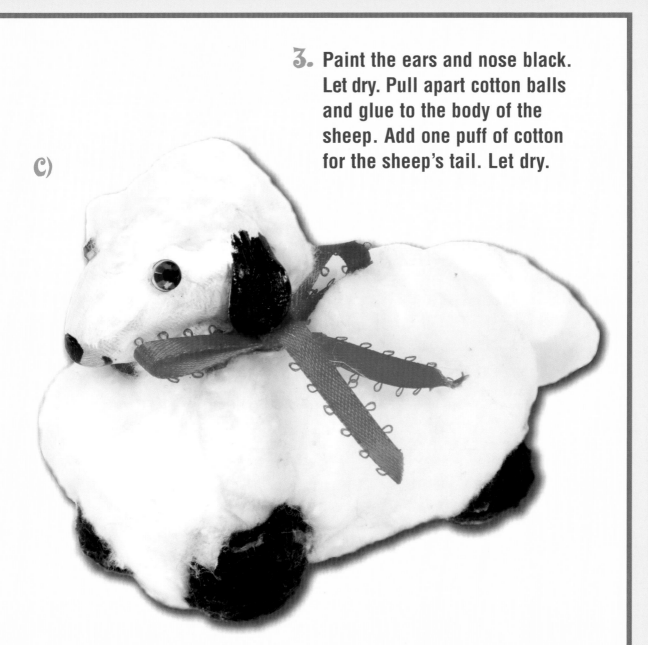

4. Cover one of the sheep's legs in glue. Wind black yarn around the leg until it is covered. Cut the yarn. Repeat for the rest of the legs. Let dry. Tie a piece of red ribbon around the sheep's neck (See C).

UTAH

Origin of name	The name Utah comes from the Ute Indians. *Ute* means "people of the mountains."
Flag	The state flag of Utah is blue, edged in gold fringe. The state seal appears in the center. Two sego lilies, symbols of peace, flank a beehive. The beehive represents industry. The American bald eagle is a symbol of protection during war and times of peace. Two United States flags surround the beehive and lilies. The state motto, "Industry," appears over the beehive. Beneath the beehive is the state's name in white letters, with the dates 1847 and 1896. In 1847, Brigham Young settled the Mormon church, or the Church of Jesus Christ of Latter-day Saints, in Utah. In 1896, Utah became a state.
Capital	Salt Lake City

Nickname	**The Beehive State**
Motto	**"Industry"**
Size (in area)	**13th largest**
Animal	**Rocky Mountain elk**
Bird	**California gull**
Flower	**sego lily**
Gem	**topaz**
Tree	**blue spruce**
Fish	**Bonneville cutthroat trout**
Industry	**computer software, mining, tourism, food processing, cattle, dairy, poultry, hay**

PETROGLYPH HEADBAND

At Newspaper Rock near Canyonlands National Park, there are ancient petroglyphs that show many people and animals. A petroglyph is a picture made by using a sharp instrument to carve or etch into a rock. There are more than six hundred fifty pictures on Newspaper Rock. Some are about two thousand years old.

What you will need

* poster board
* ruler
* scissors
* black permanent marker
* colored markers
* clear tape

What you will do:

1. Cut a strip of poster board that is 3 1/2 inches wide and 22 inches long.

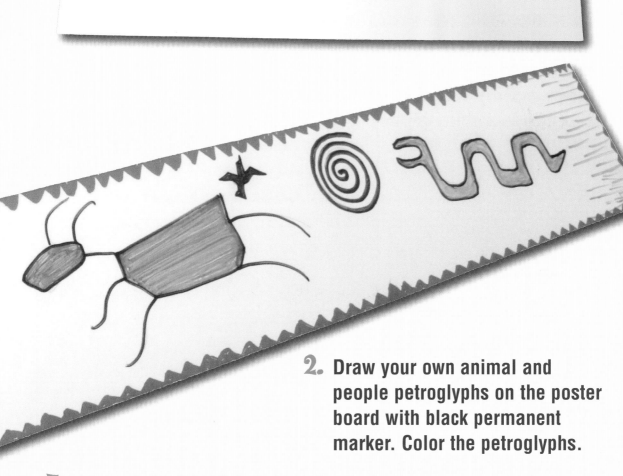

2. Draw your own animal and people petroglyphs on the poster board with black permanent marker. Color the petroglyphs.

3. Ask an adult to help you cut the headband so that it fits around your head with two extra inches. Fit the headband to your head, and tape it to the right size.

SEA MONSTER BOAT

Long ago, the Shoshone Indians who lived in the Bear Lake area of Utah saw a ninety-foot-long brown creature. It looked like a huge snake with small legs. Since then, other people said they saw the monster too. There is even a legend that says the sea monster used to carry people away. At Garden City on the shore of Bear Lake, you can take a ride on a boat shaped like a sea monster!

What you will need

* self-hardening clay
* rhinestones
* poster paint
* paintbrush
* glitter pens

What you will do:

1. Use your imagination and some self-hardening clay to make a sea monster boat. It can look any way you like. Press rhinestones into the clay (See A). Let dry.

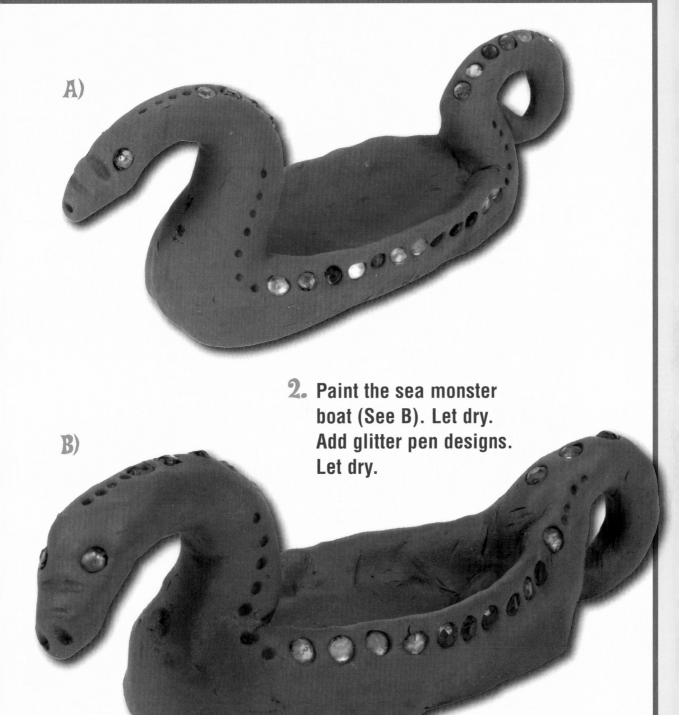

A)

B)

2. Paint the sea monster
boat (See B). Let dry.
Add glitter pen designs.
Let dry.

NEVADA

Origin of name	Nevada comes from the Spanish word meaning "snow-covered."
Flag	The Nevada state flag is blue, with two sprays of sagebrush in the top-left corner. In between the sagebrush is a silver star, with one point up. "Nevada" is printed below the star and above the sagebrush. A scroll with the phrase "Battle Born" appears in black letters over the sagebrush in a gold scroll.
Capital	Carson City
Nickname	The Sagebrush State

Motto	"All for Our Country"
Size (in area)	7th largest
Animal	desert bighorn sheep
Bird	mountain bluebird
Fish	Lahontan cutthroat trout
Flower	sagebrush
Tree	single-leaf piñon and bristlecone pine
Industry	gambling, ranching, mining, tourism

Nevada

MINI WOODEN SKIS FRIDGE MAGNET

John "Snowshoe" Thompson learned to ski when he was a young boy in Norway. In 1855, when he was about twenty-eight years old, Thompson heard that the U.S. Postal Service needed someone to deliver the mail during bad winter weather. Some people had to wait much too long to get their mail. Thompson used his homemade oak skis to deliver mail to the mines and towns in California and Nevada in the Lake Tahoe area. He carried a heavy mail sack that sometimes weighed one hundred pounds!

What you will need

* white glue
* water
* poster paint
* paintbrush
* plastic spoon
* two small craft sticks
* construction paper
  or felt scraps
* scissors
* strip magnet

What you will do:

1. Mix 1 tablespoon of glue with 1 1/2 tablespoons of water. Add 1 teaspoon of brown poster paint. Stir with a plastic spoon. Paint two craft sticks. Let dry.

2. Cut two 1/4-inch-long x 1/4-inch-wide strips of construction paper. Glue each strip to the middle of each ski. Let dry. Use paint to make a design on the skis. Let dry. Glue one ski on top of the other, so that the skis form an X. Let dry.

3. Glue magnets on the back. Let dry. Place on the refrigerator.

GLASS HOUSE CRAFT

In 1905, Tom Kelly built a house made of bottles in Rhyolite, Nevada. He used adobe, which is clay mixed with straw, and thousands of bottles to build the house. There are only a few buildings left standing in Rhyolite. But visitors still come to the town to see Tom Kelly's unusual house made of bottles.

What you will need

* scissors
* 1/2-pint carton
* ruler
* terra cotta self-hardening clay
* plastic knife
* small glass gems or plastic beads
* green construction paper or stiff felt
* white glue

What you will do:

1. Cut a door shape into the carton. Set aside. Roll out a piece of clay to about 5 inches wide, 16 inches long, and 1/8 inch thick. With a plastic knife, cut four pieces just big enough to cover each side of the carton with clay. Press each piece of clay onto the carton, and join at the seams. Leave the door space open.

2. Cut a rectangle and two triangles of green construction paper or felt. Fold the rectangle, and make a crease in the center. Glue it to the top of the carton. Glue the triangles to the top of the carton. Let dry.

3. Press glass gems or plastic beads
into the clay. Let dry.

PATTERNS

Dinosaur Bone Treasure Box

At 100%

Use tracing paper to copy the patterns on these pages. Ask an adult to help you cut and trace the shapes.

Dinosaur Bone Treasure Box

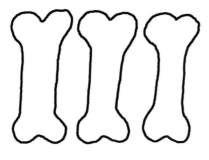

At 100%

Craters of the Moon Display

At 100%

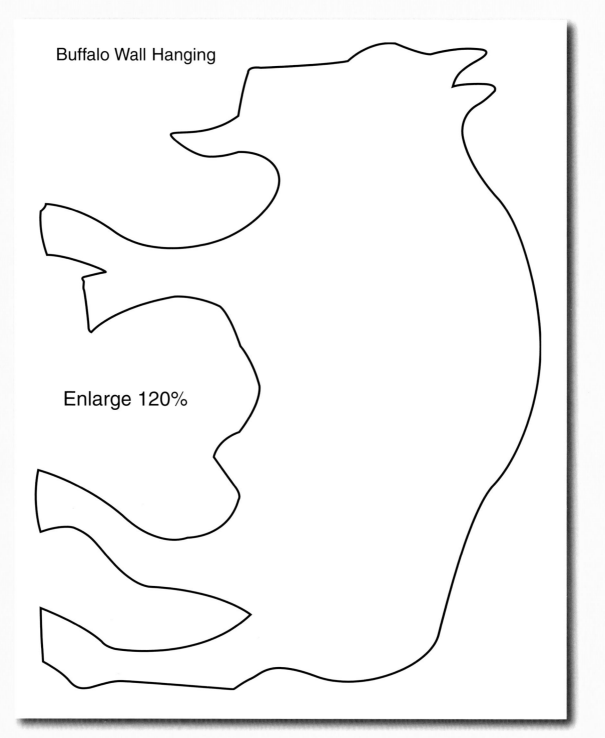

Buffalo Wall Hanging

Enlarge 120%

LEARN MORE

Books

Brown, Jonatha A. *Montana*. Milwaukee, Wisc.: Gareth Stevens, 2007.

Heinrichs, Ann. *America the Beautiful: Nevada*. Minneapolis, Minn.: Compass Point Books, 2008.

Petreycik, Rick. *Wyoming*. New York: Marshall Cavendish Benchmark, 2007.

Sanders, Doug. *Idaho.* New York: Benchmark Books, 2005.

Sanders, Doug. *Utah (It's My State!).* New York: Benchmark Books, 2004.

Internet Addresses

50states.com
   <http://www.50states.com/>

U.S. States
   <http://www.enchantedlearning.com/usa/states/>

INDEX